THE LITTLE BOOK OF
ROUTE 66

Published in 2022 by OH!
An Imprint of Welbeck Non-Fiction Limited,
part of Welbeck Publishing Group.
Based in London and Sydney.
www.welbeckpublishing.com

Disclaimer:
This book is intended for general informational purposes only and should not
be relied upon as recommending or promoting any specific practice, diet or
method of treatment. It is not intended to diagnose, advise, treat or prevent
any illness or condition and is not a substitute for advice from a professional
practitioner of the subject matter contained in this book. You should not use the
information in this book as a substitute for medication, nutritional, diet, spiritual
or other treatment that is prescribed by your practitioner. The publisher makes
no representations or warranties with respect to the accuracy, completeness or
currency of the contents of this work, and specifically disclaim, without limitation,
any implied warranties of merchantability or fitness for a particular purpose and
any injury, illness, damage, death, liability or loss incurred, directly or indirectly
from the use or application of any of the contents of this book. Furthermore, the
publisher is not affiliated with and does not sponsor or endorse any uses of or
beliefs about in any way referred in this book.

ISBN 978-1-80069-175-9

Compiled and written by: Malcolm Croft
Editorial: Vicroria Godden
Project manager: Russell Porter
Design: Tony Seddon
Production: Rachel Burgess

A CIP catalogue record for this book is available from the British Library

Printed in China

10 9 8 7 6 5 4 3 2 1

Illustrations: Freepik.com

THE LITTLE BOOK OF

ROUTE 66

THE ULTIMATE ROAD TRIP

CONTENTS

INTRODUCTION

Welcome to Route 66! From Illinois' Land of Lincoln to California's Wild West, and everything in between, this 2,400-mile slice of all-you-can-eat Americana is the best way to see the real United States. Because uniting the states is what Route 66 always did best.

Route 66 may have connected the east to west literally, but it also united the old with the new, the red with the blue, the sun with the snow. Yes, Route 66 was more than just a road. It represented everything that is good about America. It's hard not to get romantic about it.

The people's highway, the road of dreams, the great diagonal way, America's Main Street, the Mother Road, the Will Rogers Highway—Route 66 is known as so many things to so many people. It's the highway that represented America's fast rise to superpower; it drove the nation to fall in love with cars; it's original billboard advertising sold the nation on its own love of consumerism and promised gold at the end of the rainbow—Hollywood. Route 66 is a symbol of America's manifest destiny, the American Dream. But like all dreams, it ended. And the very thing that made Route 66 great, also killed it: progress.

Since being decommissioned in 1985, Route 66 has remained a beacon of all that became great about the states—motels, all-day breakfast, drive-ins, neon signs, extra-large everything. Today, Route 66 remains a pilgrimage for millions of travelers and dreamers, who seek to remember a future full of possibility. During its 1940–1970 heyday, Route 66 epitomized the spirit of what it was to be an American, a concept that it is now so woven into the culture of its peoples that the idea of ever losing it would be too much to bear.

The Little Book of Route 66 keeps the dream alive. It is the perfect driving companion to help fix your fix for Route 66, a tiny tome to leave at home, or a bitesize book to throw in your glove compartment, ready to jump into action on your next Route 66 adventure.

So, get your motor running, and head out on the highway, onto the road of dreams. Let's get our kicks on Route 66...

ROUTE 66

CHAPTER ONE

Hit the Road, Jack

Are you ready for the road trip of a lifetime? If so, buckle up and turn the classic road tunes loud enough to get your motor running. It's time to hit the road, Jack. There's no turning back.

Start of the Trail

The official starting line for travelers heading west on Route 66 is outside the now world-famous Lou Mitchell's Café, at the intersection of boulevards Jackson and Jefferson.

Jackson Boulevard was the starting point for the original Route 66, and Lou's has been feeding hungry dreamers and drivers with all-day breakfast since it opened in 1923.

Road Classics: Playlist #1

Road trippin' Route 66? Set your playlist to stun with these classic drivin' tunes, each one hand-chosen to get your motor running as you head out on the highway.

1 "Born to Be Wild," Steppenwolf
2 "Running on Empty," Jackson Browne
3 "Road Trippin'," Red Hot Chili Peppers
4 "Fast Car," Tracy Chapman
5 "Road to Nowhere," Talking Heads
6 "Life Is a Highway," John Cochrane
7 "Mustang Sally," Wilson Pickett
8 "Don't Stop Believing," Journey
9 "American Pie," Don McLean
10 "Bright Side of the Road," Van Morrison

"

They're driving
right by, they don't
even know what
they're missing.

"

About Route 66, Lightning McQueen, *Cars* (2006)

Will Rogers

In 1952, Route 66 became officially known as the Will Rogers Highway, in honor of Will Rogers, Oklahoma's favorite son, the comedian, actor, and political commentator, born in 1879. In the late 1890s, Rogers left his Cherokee ancestral home and headed west on the cattle route that would become Route 66 to pursue a career in Hollywood. He became a star and spent his life praising his literal road to fame, mythologizing the importance of Route 66 into popular culture. A plaque along Route 66 is dedicated to Rogers: "Highway 66 was the first road he traveled in a career that led him straight to the hearts of his countrymen."

Beale's Wagon Road, Part One

Before Route 66 was born to be wild, it was a cattle and wagon trail that followed the thirty-fifth parallel—the circle of latitude that runs 35 degrees north of the earth's equatorial plane. The route was first established in October 1857 when Lieutenant Edward Fitzgerald Beale was tasked by Ulysses S. Grant—military leader and eighteenth president of the United States (1869–1877)—to devise a trade route along the parallel.

Beale would later achieve national fame in 1848 when he carried the very first gold samples from California to the east. By doing so, he kickstarted the nation's Gold Rush.

Top Ten Things to See on Route 66: Illinois

1 Route 66 start- and end-point signs, Chicago
2 Ambler's Texaco Gas Station, Dwight
3 Historic Standard Oil Gasoline Station, Odell
4 Mural City, Pontiac
5 Sprague's Super Service Station, Normal
6 Ariston Café, Litchfield
7 Lauterbach Muffler Man, Springfield
8 Soulsby's Shell Service Station, Mt. Olive
9 Historical Chain of Rocks Bridge, Madison
10 World's Largest Covered Wagon, Lincoln

Eat Me: Illinois

When in Rome, eat as the Romans do. When on Route 66, eat as Americans do … so why not try the official state dishes of the highway's ate, oops, *eight* states.

Chicago is home, obviously, to the deep-dish pizza, but did you know that Illinois is one of the world's top popcorn makers? Popcorn is the state food of Illinois.

America's Main Street

The father of Route 66, Charles Avery,
and Route 66 architect, John Woodruff,
were chairmen of the national
U.S. Highway 66 Association. The
organization had two goals: promote the
road and get it paved.

At the first press conference marketing
the road, in 1926, Avery coined the
phrase "The Main Street of America" and
the slogan proved efficient. Suddenly,
general stores, gas stations, and diners
were lined up along the road making
Route 66 the Main Street in each of the
300 towns it once passed through.

Forrest Gump's Route 66

In the iconic movie of the same name, Forrest Gump famously ran for 3 years, 2 months, 14 days, and 16 hours, running 15,248 miles, crossing the United States five times.

Between Forrest's first stop in Los Angeles, and his second stop at Marshall Point Lighthouse in Maine, Forrest ran the entire length of Route 66! He came to a stop in Monument Valley, Utah.

Side note: On Santa Monica Pier, the spiritual western terminus of Route 66, there is a Bubba Gump Shrimp restaurant.

Mc66

The first ever McDonald's* restaurant opened in 1948 in San Bernardino, California, along—yes, you guessed it—Route 66!

Brothers Dick and Mac McDonald established the hamburger restaurant using their world-first fast-food delivery system. A hamburger cost 15 cents.

Today, the site is home to the McDonald's Route 66 Museum.

*The first McDonald's operated by Ray Kroc (the man who later bought the business from the McDonald brothers) opened in Illinois in 1955—the first state on the trip west from Chicago, also along Route 66.

At the Drive-In: Top Ten Classic Road Trip Movies

Road trips are the ideal way to see all the wonderful and wildly diverse wilderness the nation has to offer. Are these the best American road trip movies? Yes…

1 It Happened One Night (1934)
2 Sullivan's Travels (1941)
3 Easy Rider (1969)
4 National Lampoon's Vacation (1983)
5 Planes, Trains and Automobiles (1987)
6 Rain Man (1988)
7 Midnight Run (1988)
8 Thelma & Louise (1991)
9 True Romance (1993)
10 The Muppet Movie (1979)

Mississippi River

Cutting Route 66 in half vertically, the Mississippi River is almost exactly the same length as Route 66. It flows 2,350 miles from its source at Lake Itasca, Minnesota, through the center of the continental United States to the Gulf of Mexico, making it the fifteenth largest river in the world. More importantly, the Mississippi is also considered a cultural curtain, dividing the U.S. east from the west.

Eat Me: Missouri

Missouri, the Show-Me State, adopted the ice cream cone as its state dessert, ever since it invented it for the now-famous World's Fair, St. Louis, in 1904. So, when driving through Missouri, stop and get your licks (of ice cream) on Route 66.

First Drive-Thru

The world's first drive-thru restaurant—the unbeatable combo of car and fast food—is believed to be Red's Giant Hamburg, Springfield, Missouri. It was, of course, an icon of Route 66. Red's legendary, and infamous, roadside sign was a massive cross that spelled the words "Giant Hamburg." It opened in 1947 and closed for good in 1984, a year before Route 66 was decommissioned.

Federal Aid Highway Act of 1921

Before Route 66 and other highways were established in the 1920s, a road assessment taken in 1911 estimated the total mileage of rural roads in America at approximately 2.5 million miles, only 10 percent of which were paved.

The Federal Aid Highway Act of 1921 was designed to create a drivable highway network that allowed things called "automobiles" a nice smooth ride and that gave horse-drawn carts a well-earned rest.

Route 66 State Population Totals

Each of Route 66's eight states enjoyed surges in tourism and residential populations* during the 1950s and 1960s heyday, none more so than California.

	1926	Today
California	4.29	39.7
Illinois	7.40	12.85
Missouri	3.56	6.16
Oklahoma	2.26	3.97
New Mexico	.403	2.1
Arizona	.403	7.2
Texas	5.45	29.2
Kansas	1.84	2.95

* All values in the table are in millions

Route 66 at Large #1

Everything America does is bigger and better than everywhere else. It was only fitting that, during Route 66's tenure as the best road in the world, it attracted the world's biggest—literally, huge— roadside attractions.

Welcome to Tulsa, Oklahoma. The former "Oil Capital of the World" has the world's largest statue of an oil-driller. At 76 feet tall, the Golden Driller is the sixth tallest statue in the U.S.

A Road by Any Other Name

The road of dreams, opportunity, freedom, and the highway of hope is also known by several other revered nicknames.

The Great Diagonal Way

Route 66 received this moniker because a large section of the highway (Chicago to Oklahoma City) ran diagonally, unlike the other highways.

The Mother Road

Coined by John Steinbeck in *The Grapes of Wrath* (1939), the road was so-named because it beckoned to migrants moving west in search of work.

The Main Street of America

The U.S. Highway 66 Association used this nickname to advertise the highway.

The Will Rogers Highway

Named officially Will Rogers Highway in 1952 in honor of Will Rogers, comedian and actor.

ROUTE 66

CHAPTER TWO

New Frontier

Heading to California from Chicago means we've got a long way to go. Thankfully, Route 66 is jam-packed with a wealth of wonderful landmarks and wild landscapes to keep the eyes peeled to the road. What spot will you see first that makes you want to stop?

Icons of 66

As ranked by the website route66.com in 2015, the top ten icons of Route 66 are as follows. If you miss them, you'll miss out.

1 Jack Rabbit Trading Post, near Joseph City, Arizona
2 Big Texan Steak Ranch, Amarillo, Texas
3 Ted Drewes Frozen Custard, St. Louis
4 Old Chain of Rocks Bridge, St. Louis
5 Munger Moss Motel, Lebanon, Missouri
6 Wigwam Motel, San Bernardino, California
7 Petrified Forest National Park, Arizona
8 Midpoint Café, Adrian, Texas
9 Meteor Crater, Arizona
10 Oatman, Arizona

The ghost town of
Radiator Springs in
Pixar's film *Cars* (2006)
is based on Peach
Springs, Arizona,
along Route 66.

> **"**
> All he needed
> was a wheel in his
> hand and four on
> the road.
> **"**

Jack Kerouac, *On the Road* (1957)

Songs about Roads: Playlist #2

No road trip is complete without a
themed playlist of songs.

1 "Hit the Road, Jack," Ray Charles
2 "Middle of the Road," The Pretenders
3 "Thunder Road," Bruce Springsteen
4 "End of the Road," Boyz II Men
5 "Take Me Home, Country Roads,"
John Denver
6 "Goodbye Yellow Brick Road," Elton John
7 "The Long and Winding Road,"
The Beatles
8 "Long Road to Ruin," Foo Fighters
9 "Country Road," James Taylor
10 "On the Road Again," Willie Nelson

The Ariston Café

The longest-operating restaurant along Route 66 is the Ariston Café—and it's still open for business. Located in Litchfield, Illinois, and established along Route 66 in 1935, Ariston Café was added to the U.S. National Register of Historic Places in 2006. Their classic burger is a Route 66 tradition—but the All American Favorite Hot Beef Sandwich is out of this world.

If you fancy a hot dog, dipped in batter, deep fried, and served on a stick, then drive immediately to the Cozy Dog Inn in Springfield, Illinois— the home of this now-iconic, Route 66 treat since 1949. Same original recipe, same strangely delicious taste!

In the years following the end of World War II, the American population shifted from the snowbelt states of the east to the sunbelt states of the west.

Census figures show that the population along Route 66 surged 40 percent in New Mexico and 74 percent in Arizona.

Motel Stops

In 1929, three years after the opening of Route 66, motorist hotels (motels) sprang up to accommodate sleepy and weary travelers on the road of dreams. From effectively zero in 1926, America was about to see a rise in motel-mania.

Motels by State in 1929

Illinois	**968**	Missouri	**491**
Arizona	**93**	Oklahoma	**346**
New Mexico	**61**	Texas	**673**
Kansas	**219**	California	**1,455**

From 1929 to 1948, more than 30,000 motels opened for business along the nation's flourishing highways.

At the Drive-In

Despite the fact that less than 8 percent of America's drive-in theaters have survived, during the heyday of Route 66 in the 1950s and 1960s, drive-ins were as iconic as the road that housed them. Nothing else could better blend two of America's great loves together: cars and movies.

The 66 Drive-In, located in Carthage, Jasper County, Missouri, opened on September 22, 1949, and is now regarded as Route 66's historic drive-in theater. In the 1950s and 1960s, there were approximately 4,000 drive-ins across America.

Route 66 Wild Life

Bored of the License Plate Game? Amuse the family with a new distraction: See the State Mammals. Route 66 cuts through all of America's great wildernesses—cities, prairies, deserts, mountains, forests—so why not see if you can I-spy these great mammals as you pass through Route 66's eight states.

1 Arizona:
Ring-tailed cat

2 New Mexico:
Black bear

3 California:
Grizzly bear

4 Illinois:
White-tailed deer

5 Kansas:
Bison

6 Missouri:
Missouri mule

7 Oklahoma:
Buffalo

8 Texas:
Armadillo

"

And just like that, we're on our way to everywhere.

"

Emery Lord, *Open Road Summer* **(2014)**

Ford's Model T

Henry Ford's Model T was, without a doubt, the most common car first to test the new asphalt on Route 66. After all, from 1920 to 1926, the Model T was responsible for 47 percent of all new car sales in the U.S., more than 15 million vehicles.

Henry Ford famously said of his era-defining automobile that it was targeted at the common man, and the Model T was indeed the very first affordable car. In 1925, a Model T would set drivers back just $300 dollars ($4,500 in today's money).

"

Any customer can have a car painted any color that he wants so long as it is black.

"

Henry Ford, about the Ford Model T

"

Route 66 became a river of migrants flowing westward from the shriveled lands of Oklahoma, Texas, and Arkansas toward promise and prosperity in California and the West. The road west was rough and vulnerable to the elements, making the trek challenging and often hazardous.

"

Jim Ross, *Oklahoma's Mother Road* (1995)

According to *Forbes* in 2019, road tripping across America was up

64 percent

since 2015. Also, road trips (of 250 miles or more) in 2021 increased 35 percent compared to the same period of time in 2019.

Top Ten Things to See on Route 66: Oklahoma

1 Round Barn, Arcadia
2 Hole in the Wall, Conoco Station, Commerce
3 Route 66 Museum, Clinton
4 Ribbon Road, Miami to Afton
5 Coleman Theater, Miami
6 Dairy King, Commerce
7 Rock Café, Stroud
8 Blue Whale, Catoosa
9 The World's Largest Totem Pole, Foyil
10 Brick Paved Broadway Street, Davenport

State Nicknames

Why not amuse your family as you roll down Route 66 by seeing who can guess the official state nicknames of the eight states? Bonus points for anyone who can accurately name the state capitals.

	Nickname	Capital
Arizona	Grand Canyon State	Phoenix
California	Golden State	Sacramento
Illinois	Prairie State	Springfield
Kansas	Sunflower State	Topeka
Missouri	Show-Me State	Jefferson City
New Mexico	Sunshine State	Santa Fe
Oklahoma	Sooner State	Oklahoma City
Texas	Lone Star State	Austin

66

America's highways, roads,
bridges, are an indispensable
part of our lives. They link
one end of our nation to
the other. We use them each
and every day, for every
conceivable purpose.

99

Christopher Dodd

❝

You just have to keep driving down the road. It's going to bend and curve and you'll speed up and slow down, but the road keeps going.

❞

Ellen DeGeneres

On the Road: Playlist #3

Many famous Route 66 hotspots have been
namechecked in the world's most iconic songs.
As you drive through these destinations, stop,
rock, and roll to the roadmap of Route 66.

1 "Take It Easy," The Eagles
2 "(Is This the Way to) Amarillo," Tony Christie
3 "(Get Your Kicks on) Route 66," Chuck Berry
4 "Our Town," James Taylor
5 "Sweet Home Chicago," Blues Brothers
6 "Long Way from L.A.," Canned Heat
7 "Hotel California," The Eagles
8 "King of Rock and Roll," Prefab Sprout
9 "'Viva Las Vegas," Elvis Presley
10 "California Dreamin'," The Mamas and
the Papas

Father of Route 66

Oklahoma gas-and-oil businessman, and State Highway Commissioner, Cyrus Avery, was the driving force behind the creation of Route 66. Today, he is now revered as the "Father of Route 66."

As highway commissioner, Avery advocated for a single roadway to link America's industrial Midwest with the Golden State, California. By doing so, his state, and his personal oil businesses, boomed. It was Cyrus Avery who coined the phrase, "The Main Street of America" in 1927.

Great Depression

In the 1920s, America's prairies, including four Route 66 states—Kansas, Oklahoma, Texas, and New Mexico—experienced the perfect storm of catastrophe: a devastating national economic depression and deadly dust storms (caused by poor farming techniques). These two tragic events caused more than 200,000 Oklahomans, Kansans, Texans, and New Mexicans to hitch a ride on Route 66 to the land of milk and honey, California, in the hope of starting a new life. It is estimated only 8 percent of travelers remained in the Golden State.

Bunion Derby

In March 1928, Charles C. Pyle, a member of the Route 66 Association, established a trans-American mega-marathon in order to promote the nation's newest highway. It was dubbed the "Bunion Derby."

The first runner to cross the country on Route 66—a distance of more than 2,400 miles—would win the $25,000 prize ($385,000 today). Two hundred runners competed. Only 55 finished.

Cherokee Andy Payne won the race with a time of 573 hours, 4 minutes, 34 seconds. "Think of the fame it will bring when I am declared winner of the greatest footrace in the history of the world!" Payne said ahead of the race.

For the first twelve years of its existence, only 800 of Route 66's 2,400 miles were paved. The rest were dust and dirt tracks, making for very bumpy riding. The highway was fully paved in 1938.

Route of Wrath #1

66

Highway 66 is the main migrant road. 66—the long concrete path across the country, waving gently up and down on the map, from Mississippi to Bakersfield—over the red lands and the gray lands, twisting up into the mountains, crossing the Divide and down into the bright and terrible desert, and across the desert to the mountains again, and into the rich California valleys.

99

John Steinbeck, *The Grapes of Wrath* (1939)

Route 66 traverses diagonally through eight states. Traveling east to west, what is the order in which you would pass through these towns?

Flagstaff, Arizona

Albuquerque, New Mexico

Springfield, Illinois

Tulsa, Oklahoma

Barstow, California

Winona, Arizona

Gallup, New Mexico

San Bernardino, California

Amarillo, Texas

* Springfield, Tulsa, Amarillo, Albuquerque, Gallup, Winona, Flagstaff, Barstow, San Bernardino.

ROUTE 66

CHAPTER THREE

The People's Highway

Route 66's footprint on popular culture is immeasurable. From music to art, movies to cars, transport to all-you-can-eat, the 2,400-mile-long road is a gift that keeps on giving long after you've turned your lights off. What piece of history will you see next?

From Sea to Shining Sea

Route 66 cuts right across the heart of America, linking two of its most important cities: Chicago and Los Angeles. Without turning left or right, the highway allows you to dunk your feet in Lake Michigan and the Pacific Ocean, as well as cross the Mississippi, Arkansas, and Colorado rivers.

Now, look up. Route 66 crosses the southern summits of the Rocky Mountains, the hills of the Ozarks, and the flat prairies Kansas, Oklahoma, and Texas. It winds through the pine forests of Arizona and the deserts of eastern California. Route 66 is a scenic tour through all of America's wildlife, wildlands, and wilderness.

Get Your Kicks

"If you ever plan to motor west: Travel my way, take the highway that's the best."

In 1946, unknown songwriter Bobby Troup was driving cross-country from his home state of Pennsylvania to Hollywood. Along the way, the idea for a song appeared in his mind. The idea was Route 66. The song was "(Get Your Kicks On) Route 66."

It remains the most covered road song in rock and roll history, sung by hundreds of artists, including, most famously, Nat King Cole, Bing Crosby, Chuck Berry, the Rolling Stones, and John Mayer.

America the Bumpy

Route 66. Near Tijeras,
New Mexico.

In 2014, the New Mexico
Department of Transportation
devised an unusual incentive to
ensure drivers keep to the 45-mph
speed limit: they placed rumble
strips along the road at clever
intervals. Driving over the strips
at precisely 45 mph, the road
"performs" a bumpy rendition of
"America the Beautiful."

Cycle the States

In May 2021, the United States Bicycle Route System completed the first section of the United States Bicycle Route 66, between Missouri and Kansas. The USBRS' purpose was to transform the decommissioned sections of Route 66 into a bicycle path that would allow two-wheelers to peddle their way across the iconic route ... and continue the great Route 66 road trip experience for the future.

An average cyclist would take 48 days to complete the 2,400-mile journey, cycling 50 miles a day.

Following the end of World War II, automobile ownership almost doubled from 25.8 million, in 1945, to 52.1 million cars registered in 1955. Route 66 gave purpose to these cars, and the highway enjoyed its peak in popularity during the 1950s and 1960s when 80 percent of all family vacations were made by car.

From 1955 to 1965, the years considered Route 66's heyday, there were 75 million cars on the road, according to Federal Highway Administration data.

❝

I challenge anyone to show a road of equal length that traverses more scenery, more agricultural wealth, and more mineral wealth than does U.S. 66.

❞

Cyrus Avery, "Father of Route 66"

Road-by-Numbers

The U.S. Highway numbering can appear confusing to non-American drivers. So let's clear up the confusion. The main transcontinental routes are numbered by multiples of ten.

North to South roads are odd numbers

These start with 1 on the East Coast and end with Route 101 on the West.

East to West are even numbers

These start with 2 (along the Canadian border) and end with 90 in the south.

The Gold Rush

America's rush for gold was forged in 1849, in California.

In early 1848, gold flakes were found at Sutter's Mill. In a rush, more than 300,000 miners and prospectors traveled to California to get rich quick, doubling the population of the state. These travelers blazed trails down Beale's Wagon Road, the nation's shiniest transportation corridor and the origins of Route 66.

Route 66 very nearly wasn't Route 66 at all. Charles Avery, the father of Route 66, wanted his highway to be designated with the transcontinental road code 60, despite the route not being quite transcontinental. The number 60 was denied by the government, who proposed 62 instead.

Avery sent a telegram to Washington D.C., proposing 66 instead. *"Regarding Chicago Los Angeles road, if California, Arizona, New Mexico, and Illinois accept sixty-six instead of sixty we are inclined to agree to this change. We prefer sixty-six to sixty-two."*

Route 66's commissioner, Charles Avery, liked the numbers 66 because he thought the double-digits were easy to remember and pleasing to the ear.

In numerology, 66 is a master number, which Avery believed translated to "material pleasure and success." Master numbers are double-digit numbers which consist of a repeating number that mirrors itself—the energies of that repeated number are thus amplified.

Ghost Town

The main draw of Route 66 is the highway's connection to its glorious past—Wild West westerns, gun-slingin' cowboys, and Americana. Ghost towns, too. Lots of them.

The greatest ghost town is Oatman, on the outskirts of Arizona, 2,700 feet above sea level in the Black Mountains. An old mining boom-town, Oatman struck gold in the early 1900s, becoming one of the last outposts of the Gold Rush.

These days, at noon, the Oatman Ghost Riders put on a Wild West shootout for tourists and travelers … right down the middle of Route 66!

Keep on Truckin'

As Route 66's infrastructure and culture grew in stature, so too did the traffic. The road particularly became beloved for the burgeoning trucking industry, which found the highway's diagonal course fruitful for linking many of the great and small farming communities. The number of trucks that traveled on Route 66 between Chicago and St. Louis increased from 1,500 per day in 1931 to 7,500 in 1941. Today, truckers move an estimated 20 billion tons of goods each year, compared to just half a billion tons in 1956, when Eisenhower authorized the construction of the first interstate highways.

Road Rage

From 1926 to 1937, Route 66 traveled through Santa Fe, New Mexico. Then, in 1927, Governor A. T. Hannett changed its course—out of spite.

After losing his 1927 bid for re-election, Hannett blamed Santa Fe's local politicians and businessmen. He wanted to punish them. So, he rerouted Route 66 away from the city, reducing Route 66 by 90 miles. It is for this reason that Route 66 *crosses itself* in Albuquerque, New Mexico, where the old and new roads link up.

Real-Life Forrest Gump

Paralleling the fictional road-running feats of Forrest Gump, Meredith Eberhart, aka Nimblewill Nomad, is the most accomplished hiker in the United States.

In 2017, the 79-year-old cross-country runner took to the road for his last big odyssey—Route 66.

"I've hiked all the major national scenic trails," he said. "I've hiked the six major trails of westward expansion, the pioneer trails … and Route 66 has just been hanging in the back of my mind."

The journey across Route 66 took him 124 days.

Birth of Roadside Advertising

Between 1927 and 1963, the shaving-cream company Burma Shave posted some 600 jingles along Route 66. Over a series of six or so separate signs, often in the form of a poem, an advertisement would unfold…

BIG MISTAKE

MANY MAKE

RELY ON HORN

INSTEAD OF BREAK

BURMA SHAVE

THIRTY DAYS

HATH SEPTEMBER

APRIL, JUNE,

AND THE SPEED OFFENDER

BURMA SHAVE

Made of Roads

Today, the U.S. Interstate Highway System is the world's longest and biggest. The total number of roads exceeds 4 million miles in total length. The nation's road network includes many of the world's longest transcontinental highways, including I-80, I-90, Route 6, and Route 20.

Today, an original
1920-era Route 66
shield sign can cost up
to $400, such is their
iconic status.

At the Drive-In: Top Ten U.S. Car Movies

The nation loves its automobiles. Before you head out on the highway, rewatch these classic Hollywood films to get your motor running.

1 Duel (1971)
2 Two-Lane Blacktop (1971)
3 Corvette Summer (1978)
4 Vanishing Point (1971)
5 Smokey and the Bandit (1977)
6 The Driver (1978)
7 The Blues Brothers (1980)
8 The Cannonball Run (1981)
9 Death Proof (2007)
10 The Road Warrior (1981)

Hotspot: Meramec Caves

Home to a cave system of more than 6,000 caves, the Meramec Caverns, in Missouri (the Cave State!), is one of the primary points of interest along Route 66. The infamous bank/train robber, the outlaw Jesse James, and his gang, reportedly used the caves as a hideout.

Today, it's
still possible to
drive about
85 percent
of the original
Route 66.

"

There's a tackiness about Route 66 that out-tacks any tackiness I ever saw anywhere.

"

Billy Connolly

The Green Book

At the time Victor H. Green published the *Negro Motorist Green Book* in 1936, Route 66 was by far the most popular road in America. Driving a car symbolized freedom. But not for all.

The Green Book, as it became known (which inspired the 2019 film of the same name), was the "Bible of Black travel" and listed businesses, from barbershops to gas stations, that would serve people of color. Following the installation of Jim Crow laws that enforced racial segregation from 1880 up until 1965, 6 million Black people took to Route 66 to escape America's south to head west.

Cars Named after Route 66 Towns

Route 66 towns have provided the inspiration for many iconic American car names.

1 Buick, Missouri
2 Cadillac, Michigan
3 Cherokee, Iowa
4 Chevrolet, Kentucky
5 Chrysler, Alabama
6 Dodge City, Kansas (in Ford County!)
7 Mustang, Oklahoma
8 Pontiac, Michigan
9 Plymouth, Michigan
10 Thunderbird, New Mexico
11 Triumph, Illinois
12 Ford, Mississippi

A Hole in Holbrook

As you enter the wild, wild west of Native American Navajo country, take a second to hock spit in Holbrook down the side of stunning Meteor Crater. More than 50,000 years ago, a meteorite weighing several hundred thousand tons blasted a huge hole in Holbrook, Navajo County, Arizona, leaving an impact zone a mile-wide across and more than 500 feet deep. Its existence caused scientists to rethink the formation of the solar system. It is the largest meteorite impact crater in America.

Six Shooter Siding

Traveling onward to Santa Fe, New Mexico, make sure you stop at Tucumcari, pronounced *too-cum-carry*. This quaint town was once nicknamed "Six Shooter Siding" due to all of the gunfights!

Tucumcari's origins date back to 1901 when it was a railroad camp bustling with cowboy drinkin' saloons and gun-slingin' outlaws. Originally called Ragtown, today Tucumcari is still home to Blue Swallow Motel, in operation since 1939 and a nostalgic icon of Route 66's heyday.

Westward Expansion

The origins of Route 66 were rooted in much of young America's desire to expand westward. They did so due to a collective belief in Manifest Destiny, a phrase coined in 1845 to enforce the idea that the United States is destined—by God—to spread democracy and capitalism across North America. There are three basic themes to Manifest Destiny:

1 American people and their institutions are special to God.

2 The United States is on a mission to redeem and remake the west in the image of the agrarian east.

3 Americans have an irresistible destiny to accomplish this essential duty.

66

Route 66 was the symbolic river of America moving west in the auto age of the twentieth century.

99

Arthur Krim, *Route 66: Iconography of the American Highway* (2014)

Origins of the Interstate

Route 66's demise was written on the road long before it was a twinkle in Charles Avery's eyes. In 1919, Lieutenant Colonel Dwight D. Eisenhower participated in the first Army Transcontinental Motor Convoy. The convoy was to test the mobility of the military during wartime conditions. Consisting of 81 army vehicles, the convoy crossed from Washington, D.C., to San Francisco, covering a distance of 3,251 miles. It took 62 days. Along the way most of the vehicles broke down, roads became impassable, and lessons were learned about the need for the construction of interstate highways. Starting in 1956, President Eisenhower decommissioned the old routes to make way for the interstate highways of the future. By doing so, he completely altered the landscape of America.

According to the U.S. Department of Transportation's Federal Highway Administration, in 2021 the average American drove around

13,500 miles per year.

This is the highest average in American history. It's the equivalent of driving Route 66 5.6 times!

* American men aged between 35 and 54 have the highest average miles per year. On average, they drive 18,858 miles annually.

Big Drivers

According to the U.S. Department of Transportation's Federal Highway Administration, these are the top ten states with the highest average miles per year, four of which belong to Route 66.

1 Wyoming: 21,821 miles
2 Georgia: 18,920 miles
3 Oklahoma: 18,891 miles
4 New Mexico: 18,369 miles
5 Minnesota: 17,887 miles
6 Indiana: 17,821 miles
7 Mississippi: 17,699 miles
8 Missouri: 17,396 miles
9 Kentucky: 17,370 miles
10 Texas: 16,347 miles

Route 66 at Large #2

In Cabazon, California, go sneak a peek at Dinny, the 150-foot Brontosaurus, one of the largest dinosaurs ever built! Diny took eleven years to make and weighs over 150 tons!

The Wigwam Motel

Perhaps the most iconic non-natural wonder of Route 66 is the Wigwam Motel, in Holbrook, Arizona, near Meteor Crater, built to accommodate the dreamers of Route 66 in the 1950s.

Tired travelers can spend the night in one of the fifteen large tepees, a nod to the Native American culture nearby. You can't miss the tepees from the road, or the neon roadside sign that reads, "Have you slept in a wigwam lately?"

The Grapes of Wrath

John Steinbeck's era-defining novel, *The Grapes of Wrath*, published in 1939, tells the haunting story of the Joad family, poor migrants that travel Route 66 from Oklahoma to California looking for work, following their exile from their home state due to the dust storms and Great Depression. The book won the Pulitzer Prize, and in 1962 won Steinbeck the Nobel Prize in Literature. In the story, Route 66 is more than a road; it is a main character, one that is filled with hope and horror. Steinbeck dubbed Route 66 "the Mother Road."

"

Nothing behind me, everything ahead of me, as is ever so on the road.

"

Jack Kerouac, *On the Road* (1957)

Big Blue Whale

The Blue Whale, in Catoosa, Oklahoma, is king of Route 66's kitsch, and one of the most recognizable attractions of the highway. This large blue whale was once a fantastic roadside hotspot to cool off on sweltering days, when it allowed swimming. It was built in 1972 and measures 20 feet tall and 80 feet long. Today, you can do as Jonah did and walk through the whale's mouth and caress its blowhole should you get carried away in the moment.

"

Roads were made
for journeys, not
destinations.

"

Confucius

66

Roads are a record of those who have gone before.

99

Rebecca Solnit

Songs about Highways: Playlist #4

When life is a highway, drive it
all night long...

1 "Highway to Hell," AC/DC

2 "Life Is a Highway," Tom Cochrane

3 "King's Highway," Tom Petty

4 "Wreck on the Highway,"
Bruce Springsteen

5 "Lost Highway," Willie Nelson

6 "Highway 61 Revisited," Bob Dylan

7 "Heading out to the Highway,"
Judas Priest

8 "Ancient Highway," Van Morrison

9 "Honkin' down the Highway,"
The Beach Boys

10 "Highway Song," James Taylor

Route 66 By-the-Numbers

Route 66 was commissioned on November 11, 1926—the eleventh day of the eleventh month. Make a wish! Numerologists believe that November 11 is the luckiest day of the year due to its doubling of the "master number." They believe that 11:11 is the universe's way of urging us to "pay attention to our heart, our soul, and our inner intuition."

Besides being a number that's associated with dreams and wishes coming true, 11:11 is also the only time of the day that all four digits on the clock are the same—when using a 12-hour clock. Even weirder, the average vacation time spent traveling Route 66 today is … 11 days! Spooky.

Easy Rider

Made for the countercultural hippie youth of its time, *Easy Rider* (1969), starring Peter Fonda (Captain America) and Dennis Hopper (Cowboy Billy), is the classic Route 66 movie, a story of two men on motorbikes who go looking for America from Los Angles to New Orleans only to not find it anywhere.

The film, the first to use music from artists popular at the time, including Bob Dylan and Steppenwolf, was a massive success and ushered in a new era of new Hollywood moviemaking.

Beatle on the Road

In August 2008, former Beatle Paul McCartney and wife Nancy Shevell decided to drive Route 66 to celebrate Paul's sixty-sixth birthday. They hired a 1989 Ford Bronco and joined Route 66 in Illinois. On August 5, they stopped in Arcadia, Oklahoma—home of the world's largest soda bottle. Resident Toby Thompson was working outside when the Bronco pulled up alongside and Paul asked him, "Is this Old 66?" After a few seconds Mr Thompson realized who he was talking to, and asked, "Are you who I think you are?"

"Probably," said Paul.

King-Size Room

After a hard day's driving, head to the Trade Winds Motel, Clinton, Oklahoma, and sleep like a king. But make sure you ask for Room 21 —that's the room Elvis Presley would regularly stay in at this motel during his time filming movies in California or traveling to play concerts in Las Vegas. Room 215 is now known as the Elvis Room.

ROUTE
66

CHAPTER
FOUR

Get Your Kicks

Route 66 is an American beauty. But in order to see the wonders of the road, look up! You won't want to miss the oversized roadside attractions of all shapes and XL sizes. The road of dreams is the home of the weird, wacky, and … what-the-hell-is-that!

Halfway Point

Welcome to the halfway point of the book!

To celebrate this fact, let's tip our hat to Midpoint Café, in Adrian, Texas—1,139 miles from L.A. and 1,139 miles from Chicago. This is the center point of Route 66.

One of the longest-operating cafés on Route 66, and open since 1928, it has a slogan outside which reads, "When you're here, you're halfway there!"

Route 66 at Large #3

The world's largest ball of twine can be gawked at from the roadside of Route 66 at Cawker City, Kansas. It weighs 13 tons and contains an estimated 1,600 miles of twine!

America's Old Road

Before Route 66 and the other major highways of the early 1900s came along, the young united nation relied on the King's Highway, the oldest road in America. Built between 1650 and 1735, the King's Highway was 1,300 miles long and bonded Charleston, South Carolina, with Boston, Massachusetts.

Today, there's roughly
290 million
registered cars on
America's roads,
approximately one for
every person living in
the United States.

Eat Me: Oklahoma

The official state dishes of the Sooner State are fried okra, black-eyed peas (not the band), and pecan pie. Route 66 tradition dictates you eat this every day during your stay in Oklahoma.

The Motel

The world's first motorist hotel—or motel—was the Motel Inn, originally known as the Milestone Mo-Tel, located in San Luis Obispo, California, on the great Route 66. Opened on December 12, 1925, and closed in 1991, the motel's destination was chosen by the inn's architect, Arthur S. Heineman, because San Luis Obispo is the exact midpoint between Los Angeles and San Francisco, a two-day drive on the dirt roads of the time.

The last original
Route 66 road sign
was removed on
January 17, 1977.

Due to Route 66's huge popularity following the end of World War II, California's Golden State attracted more than 50 percent of the total population in the west between 1950 and 1980—more than 5 million new residents, according to census figures— the most rapid and sizable population development in the industrialized world.

Pueblo Deco Style

As soon as you hit the Wild West along Route 66, you may find that the buildings start to look the same. Called Pueblo Deco, the architecture style fuses Pueblo Revival, named for the Native Americans who built the original adobe dwellings, with Art Deco. This became the preferred choice for building design in the 1920s, after being first used in the El Ortiz Hotel, Lamy, New Mexico, in 1909. It was widely adopted from the Midwest to California, becoming the signature style of Route 66, particularly for motels.

Standing on the Corner

A journey along Route 66 will take you to Winslow, Arizona. Here, you'll be invited to take it easy, just like in the Eagles' iconic 1972 rock song. All you have to do is stand on the corner of 2nd Avenue (Old Route 66 eastbound) and North Kinsley Avenue, and let the Eagles do the rest. To commemorate this famous song's Route 66 shout-out, a statue was built in 1999 in its honor, comprising a man with a guitar, a Route 66 sign that reads, "Standin' on the corner," a flatbed truck, and a *trompe-l'oeil* mural. It's such a fine sight to see.

66

Afoot and light-hearted
I take to the open road,
Healthy, free, the world
before me,

The long brown path
before me leading
wherever I choose.

99

Walt Whitman, *Song of the Open Road* **(1856)**

Ye Oldesmobiles

Following the super-success of the Ford Model T in the 1920s, other makes and models soon started to appear in the eight states of Route 66. These eight were the most popular cars of the time.

1 1929 Ford Model A Deluxe Roadster
2 1920 Rolls-Royce Phantom Limousine
3 1928 Falcon Knight Roadster
4 1926 Packard Twin 6 Roadster
5 1927 Willys-Overland Whippet 93A
6 1929 Hudson7 Roadster
7 1920 Nash Touring
8 1929 Studebaker Roadster

"

Some men take good care of a car; others treat it like one of the family.

"

Evan Esar

66

Straight roads are
for fast cars, turns
are for fast drivers.

99

Colin McRae

State Lines

Route 66 runs through eight states,
each with their own slice of ownership
of the highway. From longest to least,
these are the states that have the most
Route 66 in them.

1 New Mexico – 487 miles
2 Oklahoma – 432 miles
3 Arizona – 401 miles
4 Missouri – 317 miles
5 California – 314 miles
6 Illinois – 301 miles
7 Texas – 186 miles
8 Kansas – 13 miles

Route 66 at Large #4

The world's largest thermometer can be seen Baker, California, off Route 66. On July 10, 1934, California's Death Valley recorded a temperature of 134°F, officially the highest temperature ever recorded on earth!

To commemorate the world-beating heat, a 134-feet-tall thermometer was constructed in the nearby town of Baker. It accurately displays the daily temperatures of the blistering California desert.

(Not to be used rectally.)

Eat Me: Kansas

Kansas, the Sunflower State, is the home of barbecue. Any and all barbecue. Kansas City is world famous for ribs seasoned with a dry rub, slow-smoked over wood, and served with barbecue sauce. No Route 66 road trip is complete without eating a whole hog's worth of the finger-lickin' stuff.

At the Drive-In: Top Ten U.S. Route 66 Movies

Route 66 has been the inspiration, and location, of scores of great American movies. These are perhaps the best. Question is, can you name the scenes that show Route 66?

1 Little Miss Sunshine (2006)
2 Cars (2006)
3 Easy Rider (1969)
4 The Grapes of Wrath (1940)
5 Starman (1984)
6 Beneath the Dark (2010)
7 Wild Hogs (2007)
8 Natural Born Killers (1994)
9 The Outsiders (1983)
10 No Country for Old Men (2007)

According to a 2011 Route 66 Corridor Preservation report, **61 percent** of all Route 66 drivers head west, rather than eastward toward Chicago.

Long and Winding Road

Arguably one of the twistiest and turniest sections of Route 66 is the 50-mile stretch of Sitgreaves Pass, Mohave County, Arizona. The severe switchbacks sit at an elevation of 3,550 feet above sea level and contain steep drop-offs should your eyes wander from the road to admire the mountains.

In the 1950s and 1960s, the Pass was so intimidating that out-of-towners would hire local drivers to negotiate the most perilous parts for them.

Silly Route 66

There are more than 300 towns along Route 66. Some sound a little bit sillier than others…

1 Shirley
2 Funks Grove
3 Normal
4 Eureka
5 Doolittle
6 Hooker
7 Devil's Elbow

8 Albatross
9 Rescue
10 Commerce
11 Needles
12 Bagdad
13 Two Guns

The Blues Brothers—Jake "Joliet" and Elwood Blues are named after two Illinois state towns, both of which run along Route 66. *The Blues Brothers* (1980) is one of the great American road trip movies. The Bluesmobile is a 1974 Dodge Monaco sedan. Monaco, California, is a few miles south from Route 66's western terminus.

66

Route 66 remains the highway we simply cannot forget. From the very beginning it has occupied a special place in the American conscience. It epitomizes and cuts right across the heart of America. From the skyscrapers of Chicago, through the cornfields of Illinois, the lush Ozark hills, the heartland of Kansas, Oklahoma, and Texas, the southern reaches of the Rockies, the pine forests of Arizona, the desert of the Southwest, and on to the golden shores of the Pacific, Route 66 winds its way through a marvelous cross-section of America.

It passes by small towns
in the Midwest, the arid Native
American lands, the natural wonder
of the Grand Canyon, as well as the
bustling streets of Chicago, St. Louis,
Oklahoma City, Albuquerque, and Los
Angeles. It embodies the core values
of America, of those "good old days,"
with its mom-and-pop service stations,
motor courts, diners, souvenir shops,
and trading posts. Historic Route 66 is,
in itself, an icon of American culture.
It truly is America's Main Street.

Meredith Eberhart, aka Nimblewill Nomad

World War II

At the end of World War II in 1945, millions of U.S. soldiers, and then their new families, relocated to the Southwest's sunbelt states, giving the thousands of Route 66 businesses the opportunity to prosper. The population of these sunbelt states grew by 35 percent after the war.

The Mother of Mother Road

In 1929, Carl Ditmore opened a gas station half a mile south of Hydro, Oklahoma. It was one of the first stations of its kind to open on Route 66. It remained open for business, run by Lucille Hamons, Carl's wife, from 1941 until 2000. Lucille became known as the "Mother of the Mother Road" due to her kindness and generosity, offering any-and-all desperate Route 66 travelers hot meals, gas, and shelter when times got tough during the Great Depression. In 1997, Lucille's gas station was added to the U.S. National Register of Historic Places.

Route 66 ignited the imagination of the newly-minted American motorist. To promote the road to travelers, Route 66 was marketed as the shortest route between two of the nation's natural wonders: the Great Lakes (which span Illinois, Indiana, Michigan, Minnesota, Ohio, and Wisconsin) and the Pacific Coast … as well as a scenic road trip route that takes in the Ozark mountain region, the Texas Panhandle, and the Grand Canyon in Arizona.

Top Ten Things to See on Route 66: Missouri

1 66 Drive-In Theatre, Carthage
2 The World's Second Largest Rocking Chair, Fanning
3 Meramec River, Eureka
4 Big Chief Hotel, Wildwood
5 Red Cedar Inn, Pacific
6 Wagon Wheel Motel, Café, and Gas Station, Cuba
7 Historic Rock Fountain Tourist Court Motel, Springfield
8 Circle Inn Malt Shop, Bourbon
9 Munger Moss Motel, Lebanon
10 Gillioz Theatre, Springfield

Route of Wrath #2

"

66 is the path of a people in flight, refugees from dust and shrinking land, from the thunder of tractors and shrinking ownership, from the desert's slow northward invasion, from the twisting winds that howl up out of Texas, from the floods that bring no richness to the land and steal what little richness is there. From all of these the people are in flight, and they come into 66 from the tributary side roads, from the wagon tracks and the rutted country roads. 66 is the mother road, the road of flight.

"

John Steinbeck, *The Grapes of Wrath* (1939)

Route 66: The Show

Possibly the first road to star in its own self-titled TV show, Route 66 aired from 1960 to 1964. The crime drama starred Martin Milner and George Maharis,* "Two soldiers of fortune" who rode "the highway to adventure" in a Corvette in search of the right place to settle "in a nation undergoing the cultural changes" of the 1960s. Future megastars Robert Redford and William Shatner made appearances. The show was rarely filmed on location.

*Did you know … George Maharis was arrested in a men's room of a Route 66 gas station in Los Angeles, on November 12, 1974, and charged for committing sex acts with a hairdresser.

"

The spirit of Route 66 is in the details: Every scratch on a fender, every curl of paint on a weathered billboard, every blade of grass growing up through a cracked street.

"

John Lasseter, director of *Cars* (2006)

66

During World War II, I saw the superlative system of German national highways crossing that country and offering the possibility, often lacking in the United States, to drive with speed and safety at the same time.

99

General Dwight Eisenhower, later U.S. President, on the brilliance of interstate highways, as seen via Adolf Hitler's German autobahns. It was Eisenhower, however, who decommissioned Route 66.

Time Zones

Route 66 covers three time zones.

Traveling west, Central Time Zone (CT) covers Chicago all the way through to Texas; then set your clocks back one hour to Mountain Time (MT) in New Mexico, and another hour back for California on Pacific Time (PT).

According to a 2011
Route 66 Corridor Preservation
report, 200,000 roadside
buildings lie abandoned along
Route 66.

Eat Me: New Mexico

Red-hot chili peppers, with their sweet, spicy, crisp, and smoky taste, are the go-to flavors of New Mexico.

The only questions that remain for all Route 66 travelers: Red or green chili? Hot or mild? (Probably stay away from the red chilis if you're driving.)

Road Trippin'

With the foundation of Route 66 in 1926,* car ownership in the U.S. effectively tripled, accelerating from 8 million vehicles to 23 million by the end of the decade—the biggest surge in car ownership ever recorded!

At the time, Route 66 was the shortest road by 200 miles and the most scenic route from Chicago, through St. Louis, to Los Angeles. It soon became beloved by a new group of travelers: road trippers.

* In 1910 there were just 180,000 registered vehicles in the United States.

Eat Me: Texas

Welcome to the Lone Star State—Texas! Get your chili heat kicks on Route 66 with chili con carne, every Texan's favorite meal, and the state dish since 1977. Just don't add beans. That's a Texas chili no-no.

Route 66 at Large #5

In Illinois you'll find the world's largest collection of the world's largest roadside attractions! These unmissable and hugely kitsch items are now iconic Route 66 treasures … check them out!

1 World's Largest Ketchup Bottle, Collinsville

2 World's Largest Mailbox, Casey

3 World's Largest Wooden Shoes, Casey

4 World's Largest Golf Tee, Casey

5 World's Largest Pitchfork, Casey

6 World's Largest Rocking Chair, Casey

7 World's Largest Wind Chime, Casey

8 World's Largest Knitting Needles, Casey

9 World's Largest Crochet Hook, Casey

10 World's Largest Covered Wagon, Lincoln

ROUTE
66

CHAPTER
FIVE

One for
the Road

There's nothing like
Route 66 anywhere else on
earth. The road traverses time
and history. The story of
modern America was written
here. It's time to celebrate
the journey into the past and
future. Have one for
the road…

One for the Road: Route 66 Cocktail

As with anything that becomes of great importance, there is a cocktail invented in its honor. And this cocktail tastes as delicious as it feels to slip off your shoes after a long day's drive.

How to Serve
1 oz vodka
1 oz gin
2 oz orange juice
2 oz pineapple juice
2 oz carbonated lemonade or lemon-lime soda

Make it right:
Pour the booze in a mixing glass. Stir. Add in the juices and fizz. Stir. Pour into a highball over ice. Slip into something comfortable and enjoy.

Top Ten Things to See on Route 66: Texas

1 Conoco Tower Station, Shamrock
2 Cadillac Ranch, Amarillo
3 Midpoint Café, Adrian
4 Triangle Motel, Amarillo
5 Vega Motel, Vega
6 Amarillo 6th Street District, Amarillo
7 Glenrio Historic District, Glenrio
8 Buggy Ranch, Conway
9 Historic Route 66 Segment, Conway
10 Phillips Service Station, McLean

The inspiration for Mater, the friendly tow-truck in Pixar's *Cars* (2006), was Dean Walker, chairman of the Route 66 Association. Walker was known to many for his ability to twist his feet and walk backwards!

Ghost Towns

As road trippers, truckers, and travelers head west, the landscape transforms into deserts—and ghost towns. Still, they're worth checking out as you travel through.

1 Amboy, California
2 Anaconda, New Mexico
3 Bagdad, California
4 Boise, Texas
5 Chambless, California
6 Clementine, Missouri
7 Essex, San Bernardino County, California
8 Glenrio, Texas
9 Goffs, California
10 Hackberry, Arizona
11 Hext, Oklahoma
12 Holman, Missouri
13 Hooker, Missouri
14 Ludlow, California
15 Plano, Missouri
16 Siberia, California
17 Times Beach, Missouri
18 Two Guns, Arizona

Fuel, food, and fizz are the three basic needs for any Route 66 road trip. Enjoy all three at Pops restaurant, Arcadia, Oklahoma, on Route 66. Pops is famous for its fizz, selling more than 700 varieties of pop from around the world, including many weird, wild, and wonderful flavors, such as bacon-flavored coke! Pops is also famed for its neon roadside sign—the world's tallest soda bottle—which puts on a spectacular light show every night. The sign weighs 4 tons, and is 66 feet tall, in honor of the historic highway that sits by its side.

All You Can Eat in Amarillo

If you're in desperate need of a decent meal on your way west down Route 66, head to Amarillo, Texas, the home of the iconic Big Texan Steak Ranch, famed for its 72-ounce (4½-pound) steak challenge. Honestly, it's as big as the table.

Anyone who, in one hour or less, can eat the entire steak, with a bread roll, a baked potato, shrimp cocktail, and a salad, eats for free. If not, the meal costs $72.

Cadillac Ranch

If you want to see ten Cadillacs buried nose-first in the ground, then make sure you stop and snap a picture of Cadillac Ranch, in Amarillo, Texas.

Now an iconic Route 66 pit-stop hotspot, the ranch is an art installation that could symbolize Route 66 having one foot in the grave but not dead yet … or that the love affair with the automobile offers both freedom and struggle. You decide.

Either way, it looks cool!

Top Ten Things to See on Route 66: Kansas

1 Kan-O-Tex, Galena

2 Independent Oil and Gas, Baxter Springs

3 National Cemetery, Baxter Springs

4 Eisler Brothers Old Riverton Store, Riverton

5 Historic Rainbow Bridge, Riverton

6 Fort Baxter, Baxter Springs

7 Galena Historic District, Galena

8 The shortest alignment of Route 66, 13 miles, Kansas

9 Café on Route 66, Baxter Springs

10 Litch Historical and Mining Museum, Galena

66

I love everything
about motels. I can't
help myself. I still get
excited every time
I slip a key into a motel
room door and fling
it open.

99

Bill Bryson

Fast Car

In 1920s America, if you wanted to get from Chicago to Los Angeles via Route 66 in as quick a time as possible, then your weapon of choice would have been a Mercedes-Benz 680S Saoutchik Torpedo. At the time of Route 66's birth it was the fastest production car on the planet—by a country mile. It enjoyed a top speed of 110 mph, thanks to its 414 cubic-inch (6,788 cc) inline-6 supercharged dual-carburetor engine pushing a total 180 horsepower. Vroom, indeed.

"

Never have more children than you have car windows.

"

Erma Bombeck

During the creation and expansion of Route 66, America endured the Great Depression, which officially began on Black Tuesday, October 29, 1929.

By the time Route 66 was fully paved, more than 25 percent of Americans were unemployed. Route 66 was the road of opportunity.

Classic Road Trip Games
In case your kids get bored…

1 License Plate Game: The family has to scribble down as many license plates as they can see in one minute—the winner is the one with the most!

2 Spot the Car: Every member has to choose a model of car, and mark down when they see that car throughout the journey. The winner spots the most cars.

3 Quiet Game: The whole family plays at the same time—who can stay quietest the longest?

4 Hot Seat: Someone is chosen to be in the hot seat. That person then must answer five questions about themselves, four truthfully and one a lie. The rest of the family have to guess the lie.

Top Ten Things to See on Route 66: Arizona

1 Barringer Meteor Crater, near Winslow
2 Historic Wigwam Motel, Holbrook
3 Twin Arrows Trading Post, Twin Arrows
4 Town of Oatman
5 Petrified Forest National Park, Holbrook
6 Grand Canyon National Park,
Williams and Flagstaff
7 Hackberry Store, Hackberry
8 The Jack Rabbit Trading Post, Joseph City
9 Rainbow Rock Shop, Holbrook
10 Standing on a Corner in Winslow

The average American eats at least four snacks during a five- to six-hour trip.

Fifty percent of all snacks are pretzels or potato chips as their go-to road trip snack, with candy and chocolate closely behind, at 43 percent and 42 percent.

Coca Cola is the favorite road trip drink of choice with 30 percent.

Route 66 at Large #6

If you've ever wanted to see the world's largest hammer—one that would make Thor very happy—then head to Eureka, California, and the Pierson Building Center. You won't miss it. The hammer is 26 feet tall and is a replica of a Vaughan claw hammer.

Eat Me: Arizona

When in Arizona, stop for a break and check out the chimichangas, the deep-fried burritos. The perfect blend of Mexican–American spices and cultures, the chimichanga is everything you could wish for as you travel Route 66—you can eat and drive at the same time with zero mess. Though, obviously, we recommend you stop in downtown Tucson, and take a moment to see the sights.

Is This the Way to Amarillo?

One of the most iconic cultural hotspots on Route 66 is Amarillo, Texas. Located deep in cowboy country and famed from the Neil Sedaka song made famous by Tony Christie in 1971, "(Is This the Way to) Amarillo" tells the story of a man traveling down Route 66 (we presume!) to Amarillo, to find his girlfriend, Marie. The song's original name was "Pensacola" (as in Pensacola, Florida) but thankfully was changed to this Route 66 town.

The word Amarillo is of Spanish origin and means "yellow."

Pixar's animated 2006 classic, *Cars*, featuring the legendary NASCAR racer Lightning McQueen, was originally due to be called *Route 66*. The film is a love letter to the iconic highway and the freedom of the road it symbolizes.

Route 66 at Large #7

Joining Illinois in first place for all things over-sized, Missouri has a wealth of weird and wonderfully large roadside oddities along Route 66.

1 World's Largest Shuttlecock, Kansas City

2 World's Largest Cap Gun, Kansas City

3 World's Largest Chess Piece, St. Louis

4 World's Largest Fork, Springfield

5 World's Largest Giant Eight Ball, Tipton

6 World's Largest Goose, Sumner

7 World's Largest Pecan, Brunswick

8 World's Largest Rooster, Branson

9 World's Largest Roll of Toilet Paper, Branson

10 World's Largest Soda Bottle, St. Louis

66

My 66 highway, this
Will Rogers road,

It's lined with jalopies just as far
as I can see;

Can you think up a joke, Will,
for all o'these folks

From New Yorker town down to
Lost Angeles?

99

Woody Guthrie, "Will Rogers Highway" (1963)

In the 1930s more than
17 million
cars, trucks, and buses were
added to America's roads,
increasing six-fold to
112 million
by 1970. Highways like Route
66 were the response by the
government to give Americans
what they desired more than
anything else: roads.

In 1990, five years after the highway was officially decommissioned, Congress passed Public Law 101-400, the Route 66 Study Act.

The act recognized that Route 66 had become a "symbol of the American people's heritage of travel and their legacy of seeking a better life."

"

I'm in this little
town called
Radiator Springs.
You know
Route 66? It's
still here!

"

Lightning McQueen, *Cars* **(2006)**

ROUTE 66

CHAPTER
SIX

End of the Trail

All great endings start even better new beginnings, and Route 66 is no different. At the end of the trail, here in California, the best way to continue your Route 66 journey is to turn round and head back the way you came and do it all over again. Let's go…

End of the Trail

When Route 66 was established in 1926, the original western terminus of the highway was located at boulevards 7th and Broadway in downtown Los Angeles. At the time, this intersection was the busiest in the world, with an estimated 504,000 people crossing every day.

Today, the true western end of the trail is at the intersection of Lincoln and Olympic Boulevard, Los Angeles, and not at the end of the iconic Santa Monica Pier, as everyone thinks.

The End

Route 66 was fully replaced by interstate highways, multilane divided highways that were built following straight alignments, bypassing rural towns, on June 26, 1985, thirty years after the process began in 1956.

These are the I-ways that replaced Route 66:

I-55 from Chicago to St. Louis

I-44 from St. Louis to Oklahoma City

I-40 between Barstow, California, and Oklahoma City

The Grandest of Canyons

Welcome to the Grand Canyon, without doubt the most famous roadside attraction along Route 66, and the western terminus for many tourists and travelers.

A staggering 277 miles long and 6,000 feet deep and covering more than 1.2 million acres, the Grand Canyon is simply too beautiful for words.

See it and see.

Top Ten Things to See on Route 66: New Mexico

1 Saint Joseph Church, Laguna Pueblo

2 San Miguel Mission, the oldest church in the U.S., Santa Fe

3 Blue Swallow Motel, Tucumcari

4 De Anza Motor Lodge, Albuquerque

5 Kimo Theatre, Albuquerque

6 Acoma Curio Shop, San Fidel

7 Barrio De Analco, Santa Fe

8 Whiting Brothers Service Station, Moriarty

9 Ruins of the Whiting Brothers Gas Station, San Fidel

10 Roy T. Herman's Garage and Service Station, Thoreau

Calico Early Man

Route 66 is Main Street through Barstow, California. But even this iconic highway may have to take a backseat to its other famous feature.

Barstow is also home to the oldest inhabited place anywhere in the New World, thanks to the discovery of the archaeological site known as the Calico Early Man Site. Human fossils and stone tools unearthed at this location may be the proof that show humans lived here more than 200,000 years ago.

Route 66 at Large #8

The world's largest pistachio can be deshelled in Alamogordo, New Mexico, near Route 66. The nut is 30 feet tall and was constructed using over 15 feet of concrete and 35 gallons of paint!

Down the road in Albuquerque, travelers can also feast their optic spheres on the world's largest scales of justice – 36 feet tall, but nowhere near as much fun as the pistachio!

Eat Me: California

The Golden State produces 80 percent of the world's almonds, but when it comes to a state dish recognized the world over, it is of course the avocado that California is most famous for. The state is the largest producer of avocados grown in the U.S.

Route 66 at Large #9

Take a trip down to Creedmoor, Texas, and discover the world's largest shovel.

At more than 40 feet in length, and weighing some 5,000 pounds, the shovel is made from recycled materials.

Can you dig it?

Roy's Café

Located in the town of Amboy, in the Mojave Desert, is Roy's Café. In 1959, the mammoth Roy's Café neon boomerang sign was erected and became visible for miles on the Route 66 approach into town.

The now-iconic sign remained a shining light for the town as well as one of the most defining images of Route 66. It has appeared in countless music videos. Legendary actor and pilot Harrison Ford would often land at an airstrip nearby just to go to Roy's Café for lunch—he loved their homestyle cooking.

According to a 2021 Economic Impact Study, the annual direct income from Route 66 today is $38 million from tourism, $67 million in Main Street, and $27 million in museum spending—for a total of $132 million. America's total cultural heritage tourism is worth more than $200 billion annually, and supports one in eight American jobs.

Cadillac Ranch

As you head to Cadillac Ranch, in Amarillo, Texas, play Bruce Springsteen's famous song of the same name, inspired by this Route 66 icon. Springsteen wrote the song after visiting in 1980, and used the buried Cadillacs as a metaphor about how these once prestigious cars are now on the road to ruin—much like Route 66 was at the time.

66

There is something uniquely American about the motel: It speaks to the transient nature of America itself, one enabled and encouraged by our roads and highways.

99

Hanya Yanagihara

"

A motel is where you give up good dollars for bad quarters.

"

Henny Youngman

"

Everything in life
is somewhere else,
and you get there
in a car.

"

E. B. White

Dead Man's Curve

Jan Berry, the singer in the Beach Boys sound-a-likes Jan and Dean, was involved in a car crash that left him brain-damaged and severely handicapped for the rest of his life. The accident occurred on a portion of Route 66 called "Dead Man's Curve," off Sunset Boulevard, near Whittier Boulevard. The date of the accident was April 12, 1966. (66!)

Even spookier, Jan and Dean released a hit song called "Dead Man's Curve," about that section of Route 66, two years before the crash.

The end of Route 66, near
Santa Monica, California, is the
home of the worst traffic in the
world. Los Angeles commuters,
tourists, and travelers, on
average, sit idle on freeways
for 81 to 100 hours every year,
roughly four whole days.

Hotel California

The heartbeat of the most famous rock and roll song ever written, "Hotel California," by the Eagles, is the potholes of Route 66.

"Everybody had driven into Los Angeles on what used to be Route 66. And as you drive in through the desert at night, you can see the glow of Los Angeles from a hundred miles away. The closer and closer you get, you start seeing all of these images, and these things pounded into our heads: the stars on Hollywood Boulevard, movie stars, palm trees, beaches, and girls in bikinis."

Don Felder, the Eagles

Road Trippin'

Fifty-three percent of U.S. families go on a road trip each summer.

The average American will spend nearly 23 hours on the road with the family, according to Quaker State. Along the way, they will have 19 bouts of hunger, eat 13 snacks, and play 16 car games.

They will have to deal with 16 questions of "Are we there yet?," 18 "How much longer?," and 17 proclamations of "I'm tired!"

Top Ten Things to See on Route 66: California

1 El Garces, Needles

2 Wigwam Village, San Bernardino

3 Santa Monica Pier, Santa Monica

4 Bagdad Café, Newberry Springs

5 Elmer's Bottle Tree Ranch, Helendale

6 Aztec Hotel, Monrovia

7 Cucamonga Richfield Service Station

8 Roy's Café and Motel, Amboy

9 Broadway Theater and Commercial District, Los Angeles

10 El Rancho Motel, Barstow

Planning your first trip down Route 66? The best months to go are April/May and September/October. The traffic will be greatly reduced, the sting of the summer heat will be gone (roll down your windows and smell the road), and the days will be longer with cooler temperatures.

You're welcome.

Traveling at the national highway speed limit of **55 mph**, and with no stops, drivers could traverse the entire **2,400-mile** Route 66 in **35 hours**.

66

Everything in life
is somewhere else,
and you get there
in a car.

99

E. B. White

66

This is a roadside attraction. One of the finest. Which means it is a place of power.

99

Neil Gaiman